The Rhyming Diary of Jason Smith

THE RHYMING DIARY OF JASON SMITH

E. TREVOR CATTELL

Matador
9 Priory Business Park,
Wistow Road, Kibworth Beauchamp,
Leicestershire. LE8 0RX
Tel: 0116 279 2299
Email: books@troubador.co.uk
Web: www.troubador.co.uk/matador
Twitter: @matadorbooks

ISBN 978 1785892 929

British Library Cataloguing in Publication Data.
A catalogue record for this book is available from the British Library.

Printed and bound in the UK by TJ International, Padstow, Cornwall
Typeset in 12pt Baskerville by Troubador Publishing Ltd, Leicester, UK

Matador is an imprint of Troubador Publishing Ltd

Here are stories of friends and family,
of times when I've been happy – or not;
of "DAYS", not "days" – if you understand,
when things have not turned out quite as planned:
"DAYS" that stick with me and don't rot
away like others.
But first, turn the page and find out why I'm
writing this introduction in rhyme.

It's funny, I think, what things some folk collect.
I mean, some things you might expect
like stamps, football cards or autographs.
But other things simply make me laugh –
or cry.
Like butterflies caught, killed and pinned down like
brooches.
Why?
What is the point of that?
Aren't butterflies best when they fly?
Others collect train numbers or names on lorries
or photos of the latest band to hit the charts,
only to feel sorry
when they break up. Then they start
all over again with another lot.
Where does this collecting thing come from?
Do we catch it like some disease?
Does it land on us like fleas
on a dog?
Or is it inside us from birth?
But, while I question, I don't mean to moan.
I'm a collector myself. Am I alone
I wonder in collecting **words**?
Does that idea seem to you absurd?
I love words that look strange or foreign:
fenugreek.
Or words that are great fun to speak:
onomatopoeia.
I ask you, doesn't that sound really queer?
I love words that shout:

2

calamity!
or whisper −
suspicious…
Sometimes, I love to make up words:
fanticious.
[In case you're wondering what that's all about
it's a mixture of "fantastic" and "delicious".]

But my favourite words of all − and I think you
might have guessed by now;
the words I love to use all the time
are those that *rhyme!*
So I, Jason Smith, would like to share with you
some things that I think, or have seen, or do;
a kind of diary of my life so far.
[I'm just eleven. Maybe you are
too.]
And for reasons I've just explained, you can have no
doubt
that whether I'm describing something sad, or a great
day out;
no matter what, I'm quite determined I'm
going to write my diary in RHYME!

CLASSMATES AND OTHERS

Melissa Morgan really gets on my nerves.
You would find that too
if you had to sit next to her in class
as I have to do.
The trouble with Melissa is that she's very, very fat.
I don't just mean a little plump; I mean very, *very*
FAT!
If nature means you to be weighty, there's nothing
wrong in that,
but I think it's really disgusting if you *make* yourself *very*
fat.

Melissa is always eating – no matter what she's
doing.
Her mouth is working all the time at chewing,
chewing and chewing.
She arrives at school at ten to nine, face always full
of a doughnut,
big as a football, oozing jam, mouth so full it can't
shut.
Crumbs spew out left and right like the fountain in
the square,
with jam smeared all around her lips and splodges
of cream in her hair.
She reminds me of the inner tubes I have to buy for
my bike,

and when she sits down you know how it feels when a mighty earthquake strikes.

The chair completely disappears under rolls and rolls of flab.

I can't stop her flopping onto me, so I get my pen and I *stab!*

The trouble is, she's got so much fat, she seems to feel no pain,

and anything I jab into her simply bounces off again.

I'm sure, if she went up Blackpool Tower and had a nasty fall,

she'd bounce right back up to the top like some giant power-ball.

At playtime she eats packets of crisps, mint chews and a stick of liquorice,

a sandwich pushed through the fence by her mom, with a jelly in a cardboard dish.

At dinner time, she eats one-handed; the other's stuck in the air

begging for second helpings of anything that's there.

Our first swimming lesson's tomorrow, so I hope the baths have got plenty of water in, for when Melissa jumps the pool could easily empty.

MM wore a costume today. She looked like some strawberry jelly.Everything possible wobbled and quivered from her big toe right up to her belly.

The parts not covered by costume looked like joints of uncooked bacon

and when MM was standing still, some bits of her kept shaking.

'Jump in!' said the instructor, 'and show us your best.'

I'd hardly dipped my toe in

before there's a splash and MM shot past. Like a missile she was going.

She cut through the water like a shark. You should have seen her go!

'Who's that there?' shouted the instructor. 'Some human torpedo?'

By the end of the lesson she'd got all the badges she could take.

I asked her the secret of her success. All she said was, 'It's a piece of cake.'

Then she dived into her pocket and pulled out a

bag. Inside was a cake as big as a brick.
She took a huge bite, blowing out crumbs. It made
me feel quite sick.
Despite this, for MM I have, I confess
a bit of admiration.
Her size now is not a problem;
her crumbs less of an irritation.

JOHNNY

I wish I could play football like Johnny Causer.
A kid who might become a soccer star
is always popular.
Johnny plays soccer all the time – every dinner time,
every break,
each morning, each evening, weekends too.
He's got loads and loads of friends who
buzz around him like gnats.
When I was talking to Dad about Johnny, he said,
'Stop wishing you were someone else. You'll see
whatever life holds in view
will be tailor-made just for you.

'Johnny might well end up with arthritis
while you'll become one of the world's great writers.
Or maybe, you'll both have a show on TV.
Enjoy being yourself, son.
Your time will come.
Stop thinking of yourself as some kind of geek.
Remember – you're unique.'
That's what I like about my dad.
He makes me cheerful when I might have been sad.

MR. Brown - MY TEACHER.

I like Mr. Brown on the whole,
except, of course, for his weekly test.
The other thing I'm not too keen on
is that he seems to be obsessed
with maths…
'The Lord,' Sir is fond of saying,
'made the world in six days.
Is it not surprising, then, that maths
should touch our lives in so many ways?'
Now, I like maths, but believe it belongs
in maths lessons, and should stay there.
But with Mr. Brown that's not the case.
It tends to pop up everywhere.
'Wash the paint pots, please, will you Kate?
And notice how the bubbles tessellate.
Go to the toilet? Of course you may.
Don't take a picnic, don't spend all day
meditating. Instead, find out how much water we
use
every time we flush the loos.'

'You're so slow, Ricky, you're worse than a sloth.
Jason and Melissa, will you both
find out if that could possibly be true
and how long it would take for a sloth to get from
me to you…'

I once asked Sir why it seemed to be
that his head seemed full of maths completely.
He looked at me till I turned quite red,
then looked still more, till he finally said,
'Jason, your triangular nose is equilateral,
and, while I'm not one to flatter, I'll
be surprised if, when you wipe it after a sneeze,
it doesn't change and become isosceles.'
With Mr. Brown life might be strange and full
of maths. But it's certainly never dull.

SOPHIE, MY BIG SISTER.

The number of days in a year is three hundred and
sixty five – maybe six.
And for every one of these my sister Sophie has a
box of tricks
with hair things in it,
nail varnish, stuff for lips and eyes,
so her weird appearance each morning is no
surprise
to anyone.
Dad makes us laugh though.
At breakfast he's forever saying;
'Oh, hello young lady. I didn't know we had a visitor
staying.
You remind me of someone – though I can't think
who…
You look as though you should be in some kind of
show – or zoo.'
Sophie just smiles.
She's even got a stud in the side of her nose.
When she first had it, she and Mom nearly came to
blows.
But now Mom just says;
'I knew someone once with something
similar. His was a ring and he was a pig.'
Sophie just smiles.

Sophie, as you can see, is seriously weird.
She's got a boyfriend just like her.
I wish he'd marry her. Then I could have her room
and her tele. It can't happen too soon
for me.

Sophie's looks are forever changing;
every minute of every day. So
when someone asks 'Jay, what's your sister look like?'
I simply answer, 'I don't know...'

MELANIE - MY LITTLE SISTER

I've left my little sister till last. She's
horrid, vile, revolting, ghastly.
Jay, Jay, come out to play!
Come out to play Jay!'
I hear this from opening my eyes in the morning
until last thing at night.
I spend every day, weekend, and especially holidays
trying to keep out of her sight.
Jay, Jay, come out to play!
Come out to play Jay!'
She sounds like some croaky old rooster nursing a
really bad throat,
or a cross between a honking seal, a car horn and a
nanny goat.
Jay, Jay, come out to play!
Come out to play Jay!'
I've tried hiding from her in all kinds of places,
but she's got to know them all by now, no matter
how hard I try to cover my traces.
Jay, Jay, come out to play!
Come out to play Jay!'
I've tried dressing up in all manner of disguises.
Any competition I entered, I would have won *all* the
prizes.
I've wrapped a blanket round me and tried to pass
as a monk.

14

I've sneaked off with Mom's fake fur, and Dad's
aftershave pretending to be a skunk.
But it was still
'Jay, Jay, come out to play!
Come out to play Jay!'
My Dalek didn't work at all and my scarecrow was
a disaster.
With Dad's garden canes shoved down my trousers I
could hardly move.
Melanie moved much faster.
'Jay, Jay, come out to play!
Come out to play Jay!'
All disguises I've now abandoned and hit upon
another plan.
Instead of hiding from my sister I terrify her
whenever I can.
I've gathered together a collection of scares – tried,
tested and true –
and for everyone who has a sister like mine I pass
them on to you.

- Run off when you see her coming and shout
  'Your pigtails have turned to snakes!'
- Pretend that she's become invisible – and see
  what a difference *that* makes.
- Fill yogurt pots with marbles. Hide them where
  she goes most,
- then rattle them every time she moves and tell
  her she's haunted by ghosts.
- Tell her that what a boomerang is, is something
  she needs to learn.

- Throw her doll away as hard as you can and tell her to wait its return.
- Fill both her shoes with cold vegetable soup, hide the tin and disappear quick.
- When you hear her scream go up and softly say 'Did you know the cat's been sick?'

I don't know why little sisters were invented.
The only thing they're good at is turning older brothers demented.
Jay, Jay, come out to play!
Come out to play Jay!'

GINGER - MY CAT

I'd like to introduce Ginger—
though, really, he's more orange and white.
I'm certain you won't ever have heard him, though
a glimpse of him you might
have caught in the shrubbery while from shadow to
shadow he prowls,
or writhes round Dad's plant pots, or pads across his
spade and trowels.
His fur, striped like toffee and marzipan, is easily
concealed,
and the places where he travels are never ever
revealed
to anyone.
If you keep quiet and very still you can hear a rose
petal fall to the grass,
or a lupin pod burst, or a leaf-eating snail,

or a solitary pigeon pass.
Yet, no matter how very still you are, no matter how
great your care,
no Ginger you'll see, for he slides and darts
as soundless as sunlight through air.
His amber eyes see the slightest change in his world;
then ears are twitched, tail is flicked and sharp claws
unfurled.
Sparrows hop into the hedgerows, blackbird's song
is dumb,
the mouse scuttles back into hiding, and like stones
the frogs become.
For, though he's furry and wears a coat of silk,
drinks only water – or, occasionally cream or milk,
don't mess with my Ginger, for everyone who's tried
has realised to their peril that Ginger is a tiger
inside…

TOBY - MY DOG

Toby's my dog. He's my very best friend.
When I get home from school he runs to the door,
jumps up at me, puts a paw
on each of my shoulders. He licks my face till it's wet.
'Get off!' I shout. 'Down boy, down!' and yet
if he didn't do it, I'd be sad.
He's not very big – a mongrel cross–
brown all over except for a patch
of white over one eye. Anything I throw at him he'll catch;
sticks in the park, Frisbees on the beach;
high, low, left, right – nothing's ever out of reach.
He'd make a good goalkeeper.

Toby's full of life every day.
When the postman calls, he attacks the door,
wags his tail, sweeps the letters along the floor.

When I'm eating biscuits, his head's in my lap.
A sweet balanced on his nose disappears with a snap!
He's the best dog in the world.

Toby wasn't very well this morning.
He crept out of his basket, his tail hanging down.
I saw Dad look at Mom. Both frowned.
When I got home from school, Toby wasn't there.
Mom wasn't in the kitchen, but sat in her chair
in the living-room.
She was clutching a handkerchief.
Dad met me in the hall.

He didn't have to explain.
I already knew.
'We had to do it, son,' he said.
'You wouldn't have wanted him to suffer pain;
and any treatment, the vet said, would have been in vain.
Toby would still have died.
He would have crept away
to a hedge, or ditch, or some hole in the ground
and died there.
We would never have found
him.
This way's sad but better.
We can give Toby a burial and never forget
where he lies.
He'll be with us always.'

I felt as though I would choke.

I wanted the day to disappear,
wanted yesterday back with Toby still here,
his paws on my shoulder,
jumping and barking and never growing older.
But I knew it couldn't happen.
I started to cry.
Mom, still with her handkerchief, came up to me.
'We all feel like that, love, but you see,
sometimes death, though very sad, can be kind.'
She hugged me tight and, for once, I didn't mind.
I shall never forget Toby.

Ever.

POPLARS IN OUR GARDEN

At the bottom of our garden seven trees stand in a
row.
Poplar trees.
How long they've stood there no-one seems to know,
but it must have been decades for they reach up to
the clouds.
On calm days they stand like soldiers: tall, erect and
proud.
Or maybe like shoppers queuing for bargains to be
bought,
or anglers on a pier – still waiting for fish to be caught.
But when the west wind stirs and white clouds cruise,
the poplars turn into hags whispering gossipy news.
When the wind grows stronger still, rolling down

from the hills of Wales,
of eagles, Merlin and mist-hidden rocks are the
poplars' tales.
On sunny, breezy summer days a joke with the wind
they share;
shaking like clowns, their heads circling in spinning air.
But when the nights are still and crisp, with every
window shut tight,
I gaze out at the poplars, hoping I might
see them turn into rockets and soar through the
spangled sky;
as upward, upward, upward into deepest space they fly.

But the poplar trees I love the most are those that
roar through the night,
while I dream of storms, of oceans and seas of
tremendous height:
waves tall as mountains, furrows deep as mineshafts,
with my bed a galleon – a small, insignificant craft –
that the greatest of hurricanes and tempests
will surely safely ride;
and me, dreaming of harbours, tucked snug and
safe inside.

MOM'S FLOWERS

Dad bought Mom some roses yesterday:
pink buds, tight-petalled like dresses of still dancers,
or tight-lipped secrets with few chances
of ever being spoken aloud.
At least, that's how they were last night.
But this morning each one had burst open;
a cluster of burning stars,
or mouths shouting praises they are:
a simple, joyful crowd.
When I asked Mom why they opened at night,
'Perhaps they're shy,' she said;
'or like the drama of a sudden surprise.
Whatever the reason, we are surely not wise
enough to know, no matter how hard we try.
Besides, only angels never have to use the word "why".'

BLUEBELLS

'Bluebells!' shouted Dad and stopped the car by the wood.
We clambered out and gazed ahead where millions
of flowers stood.
Suddenly, the world was turned upside-down.
Some sorcerer in a dank and root-filled cave,
holding magic, powerful and vast,
had quietly waved a bark-brown finger
and a spell had been cast.

'I'll turn this world upon its head,
the branches to be roots, the clouds the earth
and the ground shall be a wondrous sky instead.
A sky of blue like the earliest dawn
or the bluest of summer seas shall be born.'

The wood still held the sorcerer's magic.
No rustle of grass, beat of wing or bird call
broke the silence.
The stillness crept inside us too,
as, silent as flowers, standing among the blue,
the enchantment filled us all.
As we gazed down on this sorcerer's sky,
we felt strange, uneasy. Why?
'This powerful magic,' whispered Dad, 'in these flowers
was meant for eyes much greater than ours.'

LIAM'S KITE

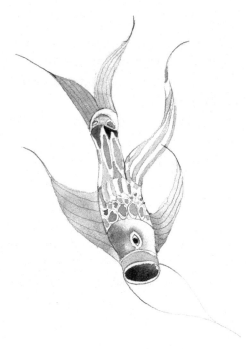

Liam, next door, said, 'See my kite!
It's a red fish in a blue sky, swimming!'
We watched it in eddies and pools and waves
over the summer tree-tops skimming.
As Liam gave his fish-kite more line
it seemed that to the sun it rose,
swooping, diving, turning fast,
scaring away pigeons and crows.

Suddenly, it was jerked from Liam's hand
by a fierce upward draught.
Some of us tried to grab it,
while others just stood by and laughed.
We watched the red fish soar to the sky
leaping and twisting to the clouds and the blue.
It circled and sailed on as though it were smiling.
As we watched, we wished we were up there too.
Later, we heard that the kite had been found in a
hedge by Liam's dad.
Liam was full of relief and gratitude.
But when I heard the news, I admit, I felt sad.

MY UNTIDY ROOM

'Jay, tidy your room!' Mom says to me.
What she can't understand
is that my room is a land
of spaceships and planets and alien beings.
'Mom, they're islands and mountains and valleys
you're seeing,
not crumpled up duvet on the floor!
And it's a waterfall tumbling from my uniform
drawer,
not a white shirt carelessly tossed away
waiting for your next washing day!
And my trainers and socks that you say you trip over
are really a test course for my model moon-rover.
The overturned chair must stay put too.
It's a tunnel that Ginger likes crawling through.
So, 'Tidy my room? Mom, I can't do it I fear.
If I did whole worlds would disappear.'
But Mom says;
'If you don't tidy up double quick,
it'll be your pocket money that does the
disappearing trick…'

ALIEN ENCOUNTER

Mark, my mate, has some funny ideas.
Today he said; 'You know Barney McGregor?'
'Yes.'
'Well, we all know he's a clever beggar.
He's good at everything – a real genius he is.
But I think there's more to it than that –
and if I'm wrong I'll eat my hat.
Take a close look at him, Jay. It's not a human
you're seeing;
I'm sure McGregor's an alien being.'

I swallowed hard, but let him continue,
when Mark's in full flow it's the only thing to do.

'One day his skin will crack and peel
like an eggshell splitting, or splintering wood.
Oozing out will come luminous blood.
His hair will slide back, underneath revealing
a purple brain, pulsing like a jelly-fish.
From his nose, thin tentacles, black as liquorice
will grow. Both eyes will gradually expand
and giant green scabs will grow on all six hands.'

Just then Barney came sauntering into view.
Quite what he was up to, we didn't understand.
He was holding a litter-picker in each hand.

He grinned when he saw us.

'Hi there you two!

I'm searching for foil – aluminium, you know –

when I've filled my bag it's off to the bank I go –

Recycling Bank – that is.

You know where I mean?

I try my hardest these days to be really *green*.'

As Barney picked his way further down the road,

Mark watched him closely, then whispered to me;

'Did you hear what he said Jay? Really weird...

He'll start to turn any day now, just you see.'

COLIN DAVIES' TROUSERS

Yesterday, Colin fell down in the playground.
Everyone heard him shout.
We rushed to where we could hear him to see how
much blood was about.
There, in a puddle and wet leaves, Colin was lying.
His face was all twisted and covered in mud, but,
obviously, he wasn't dying.
Mrs. Sheargold was bending over him. 'Where does
it hurt?' said she.
'Here, it's here!' wailed Colin holding on to his knee.
All of us pushed in closer wanting to see the gore;
a broken bone or two perhaps? A gashed knee red
and raw?
As Colin peeled away his hand we peered to see
what was there.
No blood, no bone, but only his trousers – and a
large and gaping tear…

'Is that all?' asked Mrs. Sheargold, her voice rising
in disbelief.
'My mom's going to kill me!' moaned Colin loudly
in grief.
'Mom only got these trousers last week. "Take
special care" she said.
When she sees what I've done, and sees the tear
she's gonna bash me till I'm dead!'

'I think you're exaggerating, Colin' said Mrs.
Sheargold kindly.
'Your mom will realise it's an accident and hardly
say a thing. You'll see.'
But Colin took no notice. All day his eyes were red.
He walked home, still quietly weeping, with both
feet full of lead.

This morning Colin was nowhere to be seen.
All the school was asking where he might be.
Perhaps his mom was torturing him – hanging him
up by his toes –
shoving him into the fridge till he froze,
skinning him and turning him into curtains...
Something dreadful had happened – of that we
were certain.

At midday, Colin appeared – face like a clown at the fair.
No holes, no stitches in his trousers – in fact,
sporting a brand new pair!
Not just ordinary trousers either, but a pair right out of your dreams;
designer label back and front, with fancy pockets and studded seams!
In a bag slung over his shoulder were trousers with a stitched-up hole,
put there by his mom for the next time he's in goal.
Colin stood proud as a battleship. 'Mom felt sorry for me.
When I showed her the tear, all she said was "Worse things happen at sea…"'

I told Mom how Colin's tale had ended happily.
I said, 'Mom, if I tore my trousers, would you do the same for me?'
Mom turned and seemed to read my mind; fixed me with a steely stare.
'Don't you even *think* about it, Jason my lad.
Don't… you… DARE!'

Assembly Music

We always have music as we go into and come out of assembly.

Today's music made me shiver.
It felt like iced water running down my spine,
or stars striving hard to shine
over darkening hills, field and river.
It stayed in my head all morning
and ruined my concentration.
My fractions were wrong, my comprehension worse,
until, in desperation, I went to see Sir.

'I'm afraid, Mr. Brown, you won't be pleased
with my maths or English today.'
I said.
I told him how I was haunted by the music.
It seemed daft, but what else could I say?

'Music is powerful,' Sir replied.
'Music rocks tiny babies to sleep.
It sends soldiers marching off to war.
Folk everywhere are made to smile or weep.
Why be surprised then if you cannot ignore
a piece of music?
If music can hold babies and armies in its sway,
it can easily sweep two small lessons away.'

Mr. Brown is always full of surprises.
He manages to find just the right words
to calm any crisis.
And, although I don't understand all that he said,
his words, like the music, are still in my head.

A MEMORABLE DAY

Shrieks and howls at nine o'clock today:
Why? Infants acting the fool?
I glanced at Mark. We knew the reason.
A dog in school!

Seconds later, a flash of brown and black,
coats thrown on pegs, hands grabbing bags,
while, between anoraks, ears flap, eyes sparkle;
against a sports bag, a tail wags.
'It's Demon!' laughed Mark, 'Luke Instone's dog'.
But Luke is sick in bed today.
Demon must have jumped the fence again.
He's run a long way…'
Infants are now among Year Sixers
following Demon, watching the fun.
'Mark,' called Miss Carter, 'take these infants back
to where they belong.
Jason, you ask Mr. Brown what's to be done.'

'You're both dog lovers,' says Mr. B.
'Here's a problem needing a solution.
Calculate velocity, curve of pursuit,

and – hey presto – you reach a conclusion!'

Screaming girls in the loos,
then scattering like pigeons in the square
tell Mark and me all we need to know –
Demon's in there!
Feeling a bit embarrassed, we knock, then creep
inside.
No dog to be seen, but a long row of doors
means there's plenty of places to hide.
Suddenly, a bark and a leap to the door,
Demon's in the corridor; I'm on the floor.
'Grab 'im quick!' screams Mark, face red.
'What?' I gasp, as Demon shoots past my head.

Shouts from the kitchen,
Cook clapping her hands,
Demon's nose in a paper sack,
paws in two large pans.
Mark and me strike a martial arts pose.
'You grab 'is tail. I'll grab 'is nose.'
But, ears horizontal, like pennants on a mast,
Demon dashes past.
Miss Jenkins, in Year One, at her desk is suddenly
startled
as something dives under her chair.
Her eyes turn to marbles,
her face is like plaster,
as, seconds later, covered in paint,
a blue Demon runs past her.

In her office, Mrs. Barnard sits peaceful and calm,
looking as though nothing could ever distress her.
Demon bounds in, jumps up on her desk,
and dances on her word processor.
Amazing things appear on the screen,
while Mrs. Barnard jumps up and screams.

HT*'s in his room with the door ajar,
his nose pressed in a book.
Across his floor a shadow is cast
by something or someone moving fast.
HT, from his daze has been woken.
He's annoyed, and shouts at empty space,
'Walk in the corridor! This is not a race!
School rules are for a reason – not meant to be
broken!'

But Demon's out in the playground by now.
So are Mark and me.
We've had enough chasing to last us a week –
but not so Demon – as we soon see…
While he stops at the pond for a drink and some
fishing,
we nip into the PE store for suitable ammunition.
'Throw a sack over his head – that'll slow him
down,'
says Mark. 'I'm whacked.'
I, too, had had all the running I could take
and that's a fact.
So, I grab a bag and throw it.
Big mistake…
To Demon it's an enemy or toy.
He grabs it, shakes it in anger – or joy.
All Mark and me can do is stand and stare
as we watch brown bits and dust fly everywhere.
'Do something Jay!'
'Okay…'
I take one step forward. Demon makes for the gate
dragging his sack behind him.
Great!
At least he'll be gone, I think; but, just our luck,
at that moment, arrives a delivery truck.
Demon stops, drops the sack and turning,
sees us and speeds off like his tail is burning.
We're off!
Across the field, hearts pumping again,
we see infants practising for Sports Day.

When I see skipping ropes, my heart sinks to my
boots,
feel a mixture of panic and dismay.
Seconds later, Demon's got a long rope trailing,
while infants, with shrivelled faces are wailing.
Like some Grand National horse, Demon's off again
making for the herb garden. He stops,
turns, wide-eyed and panting, looks at Mark –
and flops.

'We've got him now,' says Mark.
'The herbs will calm him – see?
They'll drug his brain, give him peaceful thoughts,
a kind of aromatherapy.'
Then Mark picks a bundle of herbs
and waves them about like a shaman.
Demon watches, ears twitching, then leaps up at
Mark.
I can't say I blame him…
Mark takes off behind the bike sheds,
Demon in pursuit.
What happened there, I don't know, and Mark's not
telling.
But, moments later he's back, minus herbs – and
yelling…
When I've calmed Mark down and he's stopped
rubbing his bum,
we look round for Demon.
He's disappeared.
We ask caretaker, secretary, cleaning-lady, cook,

but no-one's seen where he's run.
'He must have gone,' gasps Mark with relief.
And I'm inclined to agree.
So we head back to class, still breathless and hot,
ready to report to Mr. B.

'Ah! Our dog-catchers return,' he announces,
'without, I hope, fleas, bites or bruising?'
It's then we see something under his desk
that everyone 'cept us finds amusing.
'As you see,' Sir says, 'you lost the race.'
At his feet lies Demon, still and sleeping.
'Our four-footed friend seems intelligent and wise –
qualities we need in Year Six – so we'll keep him.'

So we did. Demon stayed for the rest of the day,
sleeping in lessons, enjoying himself at play.
'No different from many pupils' Sir said with a sigh.
'He'd probably do well at SATS too – if he'd try…'
'I hope he's been no bother,' Mrs. Instone said
when we took Demon home. Luke was still in bed.
'No bother at all,' I said turning pink in the face.
Then we quickly left. We didn't mention the chase.
'Mrs. Instone,' shouted Mark, 'tell Luke he missed a
memorable day!'
Which was perfectly true – well, in a way.

*HT = Headteacher

41

ANCIENT EGYPTIANS

We're studying Ancient Egyptians at the minute.
They were really strange it seems to me.
All those mummies and pulling brains through the
nose,
filling tombs with great treasure that no one would
see,
and imagining the sun dragged through the sky. It
all shows
I think, just how strange they were.
They would have *eaten* starlight if they could.
Their mason's chisels seem to have been guided
by stars that, to priests and pharaohs, confided
dark secrets.
They bathed in and drank from star-reflecting Nile
and painted constellations; all the while
dreaming of journeys through death to star-filled
lands.

Although they lived long ago in the distant past,
I know the Egyptians' starlit dreams still cast
their spell on me,
for, when I gaze at a midnight sky,
I feel Osiris, Anubis and the Pharaohs standing by.

SPORTS DAY

It was Sports Day today, and, as usual
HT talked about it in Assembly.
He talked about the Olympics
and things that made him sick
like booing and chanting
and the odd parent ranting
when their dear offspring
didn't win a thing
because the judges were blind
and, anyway, it was unkind
to expect children these days to run.
He went on to say
that it was a beautiful day,
and that 'Now we're blessed by the weather
I hope we shall spend a wonderful time together.'

I happened to glance at Mr. Brown.
Sir's face was wearing a grin.
I thought maybe he was thinking of the teachers'
race
and how he was going to win.
By half-past one we were all on the field
gazing at parents galore,
armed with cameras, videos and picnic teas,
little brothers and sisters on their knees
wondering what was in store.

HT welcomed the parents,
his voice sounding strange through the P.A.
He said he was absolutely certain
we were in for a very special day.
It was then I noticed Mr. B.,
his face, still wearing that grin.
I was going to ask him why he looked so amused,
but it was then that the Head said, 'Let's begin!'

The infant races all came first,
and were the usual farce.
With infants running in every direction,
choosing a winner called for fantastic detection
by Sherlock Holmes and Mr. Watson.
I wonder why the teachers don't just bring the cots on
and tow the kids behind them like carts.

The sprints were next, and went okay…
Mind you, Ben had a lucky escape.
The judges in charge of the finishing line
were gossiping over large glasses of wine
and nearly beheaded Ben with the tape.

Joey Benson should have won the sprint,
but was sabotaged, he said, by Rick,
who, between races, fed him rich cream cakes.
'Eating them,' said Joey, 'was a big mistake.
Instead of winning, I was violently sick.'
The sack race was as chaotic as ever.
Julie was heading home fast,
when her little sister ran on to the track
and tried to climb into Julie's sack,
and while they pushed, pulled and argued,
the rest of the runners ran past.

In the "Horse and Jockey" there was nearly a fight.
Johnny was on the back of Mike
who didn't like his jockey using a whip,
so he bent right over, throwing John off with a flip,
then sat down saying he was on strike.

The relay was almost a foul-up,
with HT in a state of shock.
One of the batons he couldn't find,
but Miss Johnson saved the day saying 'Never mind,
use this – a stick of peppermint rock.'

Vicky was ahead in the marathon,
cruising her way to the cup,
when, without any warning, her elastic snapped,
and, before she realised, her shorts had flapped
round her ankles, tripping her up.

The "Egg and Spoon" was reasonable I suppose,
though Robbie was disqualified.
He'd led all the way, egg firmly in place.
But his secret was discovered after the race:
his Blue-Tack he forgot to hide.

The Three-Legged Race was better this year,
with only one twisted ankle and one sprain.
In the Fab-Footwear Race, poor Liam fell. He
was wearing one clog and a size ten welly
and fell down again and again – *and again!*

The Dressing-Up Race was disastrous.
No one could find the right togs.
Kulvinder ran off in my football shirt,
I ended up in a sari and skirt
while the winner was Fiona Parkes' dog…

At the end of the day we were back in class.
Sir said, 'Taking part is better than winning.
My spirits are lifted – now that it's finished.
I'm rejoicing – our tradition of sport's
undiminished!'
But, you know what? Sir was still grinning…

THE STOCKROOM

'Go down to the stockroom, Jason please, and fetch me a pack of felt pens.'

Travelling down the corridor, I was Howard Carter.
At the stockroom door a voice quietly said,
'Open carefully, Jay, the air might be foul in there.
No one knows what horrors might lie ahead…'
I eased open the door and stared into dimness.
There was a room of boxes, parcels, and packages
turned into a twisting, turning maze
of corners, snickets and shadowy passages.

'What can you see?'
'Wonderful things…'
Canisters of paint stood like figures in uniform;
brushes – bristles erect like surprised hair on heads
– staring
at my intrusion. Brown walls of boxes,
like stone dungeons, were bearing
down on me.
The noises of school seemed worlds away.
My own breaths, my heartbeats I could hear.
What if the door refused to open?
I could stay forever in here.

I seized the door and pulled my hardest.
The rumble of classrooms, the corridor air
swept past me as I walked swiftly away,
giving interviews to all the press who were there.
For I, Jason, was walking away from the tomb.
I had survived the curse of the dreaded stockroom.

'Ah, Jason, what took you so long? We thought
that perhaps you were lying somewhere dead on the floor…'
'Sorry, Mr. Brown, I became distracted.
Er… what exactly was it you sent me for?'

DARREN'S HOLIDAY

Darren's just back from holiday. He'd never been before.
He couldn't stop talking about it: the sand, the sea
and shore.
He wrote a piece to go on the wall. Sir said it was very good.
He said, 'Everyone should read what Darren has written.'
So I thought I would.

'Where the sea met the sand,' wrote Darren,
'is ragged like torn paper.'
He went on to say he's
sure the cliffs are made of a
giant, white, crumbly cheese.
The patterns of foam in the waves
Darren is almost certain
are where the factory got its ideas
for the design of his mom's net curtain.
'They look,' he said, 'like pieces of lace,
then simply disappear without any trace
left behind.'
'Paper? Cheese? Curtains? Lace?'
All this seems very odd to me.
But I know that when I'm next on the coast,
thanks to Darren I'll look at things differently.

ANCESTORS

We were talking about names in school today,
and I must say
it was fascinating.
Names have always interested me.
I could never see
how some folk got their names.

For example, there's a girl living in our street–
the most miserable girl you'll ever meet.
Her name's Joy.
There's a baby too called Chelsea.
When she goes to school – you see –
grief will follow her from about day one.
Tears will follow – more tears – and then some.
Do what she may, she won't be able to fight it
because everyone here supports Man United.
And what about my cousin?
No matter what the weather is, cloudy or sunny,
he gets teased something rotten–
though he doesn't think it's funny.
He's called Max.

Sir told us that, through surnames, we can tell
something of our ancestors: their occupation,
appearance, where they used to dwell.
We listened carefully.

'Coopers made barrels, Turners worked in wood
and you can guess what Farmers did,' Sir said.
'Redheads were… well, red-headed,
Greenwoods lived near forests,
while "Driver" meant, not cars, but cows being led.'
Pargetters and Masons were explained.
Thatchers, Causers, Singhs, Sir mentioned them all.
But no Smith!
So later I complained.

I wanted my ancestors to be really grand:
great scientists working for the good of mankind,
adventurers on wild oceans discovering new lands,
afraid of nothing.
I wanted them to be authors, musicians, poets,
admirals, sportsmen, advisers to kings.
But Sir said, 'I thought you might already know, Jason.
A Smith was someone who made well…*things*…'
"Things"?
"THINGS"?
While other folks' ancestors were busy
working wonders in architecture, paintings, statues,
mine were fiddling with "thingummy-jigs", "what-nots"
"what-d'-y'-call-ems" and "what-have-yous".
Does no one know a Tutankhamun Smith?
Of a Columbus Smith has no one heard?
What about a Sherlock Smith? A King Henry Smith?
Okay… I know that sounds a bit absurd.
Perhaps some Smith was around when Noah
was saving creatures from the flood. He

would then, being a Smith, earn his ticket to sail
by making a bell for the budgie.

When, in Ancient Egypt, the pyramids and tombs
were being built by the pharaohs,
a Smith sat under a palm tree somewhere
making dice or dominoes.

When the Roman armies were sweeping across
Britain,
bringing numerals, roads, central heating,
a Smith was probably congratulating himself
on his design for a bowl to soak his feet in.

I'm sure that, while Wren was designing St. Paul's
or great advances were happening in medicine,
somewhere a Smith slaved night and day
making a cage to keep his ferrets in.

Or, maybe, while Cook was sailing the seas
on some dangerous world-circling quest,
a Smith was busy tearing his hair
designing a simple string-vest.

And I just know that when Mr. Babbage
was completing the world's first computer,
somewhere, toiling in fading light,
A Smith polished the first pea-shooter.

When the Victorians were inventing things madly,
building railways to all kinds of places,
in a tiny workshop, a Smith sat tinkering
with those things for the ends of shoe-laces.

When I moaned to Sir about my ancestors –
that all of them seemed silly and small,
he said, 'Smiths might have built bridges, or cogs, or
springs.
Where would we be without those kinds of "things"?
Machines for industry simply wouldn't go
without you Smiths to make it so.
And, in any case Jason, if you're feeling down,
pity me. Remember, my name's "Brown".'

A Serious Embarrassment

I was really embarrassed in school today.
I was sitting quietly, my thoughts drifting away –
you know how they do – out the window somewhere –
when, suddenly I found my hand in the air…
The whole class went silent. I could see
that every eye was turned towards me.
What had I done? What had I said?
My face, I could tell, was turning red.
Sir was smiling like he was a lottery winner.
'Jason,' he announced, 'you alone like school dinners!'

School dinners! I slumped back in my chair.
No one confesses to liking them. No one, not anywhere!
'Tell us your favourites Jason and tell us why
you like them.'
I wanted to shrivel up and die.

'Er… chips,' I stammered. 'I like them because…
they're the same colour as some wooden floors.'
'Floors?' Sir said. 'Floors? That reason's unique.
Do you mean that, when you bite them, they tend to…
creak?'

Ignoring Sir's comment, I went on.
'If you lay them side by side in a row,
you can tessellate them – make patterns – you know,

like the floor in the hall or some driveways you see.
Then the peas are like plants and the sausage a tree.
If your hand is steady, and you try not to sneeze,
the baked beans make autumn leaves on your trees.

Sir looked bewildered, expressionless, blank.
Round the class I heard sniggering. *He's a bit of a crank,*
I could hear them thinking, but I felt I could go
on forever, letting my imagination flow.

'Cabbage,' I proclaimed, 'is a medieval swamp.
Monsters can live there before you chomp
on them and make them become
extinct in the deep, dark slime of your tum.
Chocolate Crunch is the surface of a distant world,
and jam roly-poly, when it's uncurled,
is a skate-board park, or a ride at the fair;
or, chopped up, a staircase leading to where
there are dungeons or turrets or great white halls
where tortures take place amid blood-stained walls.

'School dinners, Sir, are great as you can see.
Ask anyone, and I'm sure they'd agree
they're better than any computer game.
Each day's a new challenge. They're never the same.'

'Well, Jason,' said Sir, 'you've given us food – for thought.'
And, grinning at his little joke, continued. 'Maybe I ought
to consider in great detail my fish and chips
before even one mouthful passes my lips.'

A VISIT TO THE PARK

Sir took us to the park today to look at autumn.
Wind-blown leaves scratched our faces, and racing
down to the grass, rested on the heads of padded adults
on benches, watching their dogs chasing
squirrels, or, rubbing their noses in heaps of leaves
looking for lost sticks.
The leaves were as bright as sunlight through church
windows,
and small birds clung to swinging wires
over bushes blazing like November bonfires.

Autumn smells like chrysanthemums in Dad's greenhouse.
It smells of soil, of wetness, of things decaying.
Ducks laugh at their own jokes, while pensioners sit
praying
that they'll live to smell another autumn next year.

I love the park in autumn;
the smell, the colours, the sights;
the ghosts in the early morning mist
and the diamond stars at night.

And yet, it seems to me strange and a little sad,
I can't help wondering why
leaves burn at their very brightest
just before they die.

A ROUTINE MEDICAL

From the first steps inside school today, one thing
was clear;
Nurse was here…
The Smell glided down the corridor like a ghost,
bringing threats of needles, tubes, strange silver
things or
a lolly stick in mouth and disinfected finger
mining for cornflakes or breakfast toast.
The Smell-Ghost squeezed itself into a thick string
and slid into nostrils and grim mouths, carrying
with it memories of visits gone by,
white overalls, black cases and 'Try
to stand still, dear…'

'You're honoured, Year Six, as it's swimming today
you're the first to be seen.
I'm sure other classes are green
with envy,' Sir said.
Everyone groaned. 'I knew you'd be pleased
to be the first to discover what's in store,
which bit of you is to be punctured, or
what parts of you are diseased.'

Standing in single file by the medical room door,
the Smell-Ghost began to bring a score
of vipers in our stomachs awake,
while smiles and stifled giggles were faked
as we pretended not to care.

Nurse appeared: blue and white like a summer sky.
'Our system today,' she explained, 'has a one-way
flow.
So it's in through this door, then out through the
Infants you go.'
Oh shucks! No chatting to those gone in before us!
Peeping through the crack in the door, we tried
unsuccessfully to discover the secrets inside,
but all we could hear was some bumble-bee chorus.

Rick, Mark and I were the last in line.
By now, the Smell-Ghost was having a wonderful time
playing marionettes with both our knees
and slicing through our hearts like a wire through cheese.
Then Rick went in…
'Come along,' we heard the nurse say,
'stand over there and put…'
Then the door slammed shut.
'I read a story once,' Mark whispered to me,
'about a wicked school nurse.
The stuff she injected put a curse
on every kid: turned them into a zombie.'
'Great!' I said. 'That's all we need!
What awful rubbish you do read!
Er… how did it end?'
'Well, when they went fishing, some creature appeared…
but the last pages were missing…'
'Well, I don't fish anyway,' I said.
'Nor me' said Mark, 'but when my uncle was on a pier, he…'
The door opened. It was the nurse. 'Come in, dearie.'
I stepped inside.

'Tell us your name, dear, and put your swim stuff on
the chair.'
'Jason Smith,' I quavered, taking a careful look
round
for signs of torture: needles, drills, any blood on the
ground.
'Stand here,' said the nurse. 'Read the card over
there.'
Read? READ? *READ?* 'An eye test?' I bleated.
I felt relieved, a bit miserable, but, above all,
cheated.
What about our nerves and worry outside the door?
All those stomach vipers – is this what they were for?
'B… b… but…' I stammered, 'what about the smell?'
'Oh, that,' smiled the nurse, 'the caretaker fell
over a tin of fluid – the one that's used
to clean the drains or disinfect the loos.'
I cringed.

'A
Y.O.T.'

I mumbled.
I staggered into the Infants feeling really let down.
Then I saw Rick
looking sick.
'Hi!' I called. 'You feeling O.K?'
'Don't mention any letters to me, Jay,'
he said.
'I think I've just made myself look the biggest fool,

the greatest idiot in the history of school.
When the nurse said, "Read the card on the wall,"
I thought it was a poem, so I joined up all
the letters like words. I read "A yacht".
Then stopped.
That's as far as I got.
The rest didn't make sense, looked foreign to me,
like Spanish – or those funny Welsh words you see
at Rhyl.
You don't think I'll have to wear specs?'
I laughed. Then the laugh spread to Rick.
We were about to tell Mark, who'd arrived, when
'Quick!'
I whispered. 'Infants coming! Let's do the old
routine
that we always do when infs are on the scene
on Nurse Day.' We grabbed our arms and pulled a
face,
whimpered a bit, lurched from place to place.
As the line of infants drew near,
our plan was working as well as ever. That was clear.
'Is it the needle?' tiny voices cried.
Some turned pale. Others tried to hide.
Rick fell to his knees, then writhed on the floor.
Mark rubbed his arm, wailing 'It's sore! It's sore!'
I grabbed my throat, pretending to choke,
when, suddenly, a deep, familiar voice spoke.

'What's this? Some reaction quite exceptional?
Some kind of seizure? Brainstorm? Can anyone tell?
Perhaps it's the latest kind of floor dance,
given, as we can see, an Oscar-winning
performance.
One thing is clear. Such behaviour shows us
swimming's far too risky with such a diagnosis.'
Rick jumped up. 'Oh please, Sir, no! It was a kind
of play;
we were entertaining the infants while they waited,
you might say.'
Sir fixed Rick with his icy stare,
the kind that made you wish you weren't there.
'Ricky Cole,' Sir said, 'I've been talking to Nurse.
So before you make the situation worse,
you should know she's told me about your eye test –
a secret I'll share with the school if I'm pressed.'
'Oh, Mr. Brown,' wailed Rick, 'that's almost
blackmail!
'It might be,' grinned Sir, 'but I bet it can't fail.
Now, there's the coach driver, I suggest you follow
him,
unless you'd prefer to stay, and read the infants a
poem?'
We didn't hang around to see Ricky blush
but headed for the swimming coach in quite a rush.
In this afternoon's spelling test – guess what!
The first word we had to spell was – yes you're right
– "Yacht"!

THE AIR-RAID SHELTER

In the corner of the school field, half-hidden by trees,
is the air-raid shelter.
A roof of concrete and windowless brick walls
trap secrets inside – memories of all
the children and their teachers who used it years ago.

It is a giant island in a lake of thistles.
Footballers paddle carefully to retrieve their ball.
Most other children don't go near at all.
It stands there solitary like a tomb.

Ignored, for most of the time, the shelter watches us all.
'It's haunted,' said Mark mysteriously, to me one day.

'Who by?' I asked.
'By children who used to play
here many years ago and then were killed in the
war.'

But this field must have seen other children-
those grubbing in black tunnels mining coal.
Or those whittling sticks watching sheep in the fold
among hills too young for high-rise flats.

I can't believe that ghosts of children live inside
among the rats, the spiders and decades of dust,
playing in darkness, or perhaps just
standing listening to the sounds of our world.

If I were a ghost, I know where I'd prefer to be,
playing on the field, or sitting with friends
in the shade of the sycamore tree.

GURDIP'S DAY

We all knew there was something different about the day.
When we entered the classroom just before nine, Sir
was not himself.
He wasn't working at his desk, nor finding books
from the shelf,
but standing, face grim, eyes staring far away.
He spoke quietly.
'Today will be a sad day, you'll find,
for last night Gurdip's mom died,' he said.
'Gurdip's feeling very upset, and frightened of what
lies ahead.
Today is Gurdip's day. We must all be especially kind.
Gurdip is not here yet, but will be in later today.
When he comes, keep most of your sympathy inside you.
Don't stare at him. When someone special has died, few
of us want our grief to be on display.
Treat him normally. Don't be demanding
of his attention. Let him be quiet on his own
if he wants to be. Let him spend the day alone
if he needs to – if not, be friendly and
understanding.'

When Gurdip came, we tried to do as Sir had asked.
We kept our heads turned away, pretending not to notice.
Concentrating was hard. Mark, on his paper wrote his
name all wrong. Usually we would have laughed,
but this time just carried on with our task.
We all tried hard to be ordinary. I know that for sure.
But I really wanted to see Gurdip, see if he had
been changed
somehow by his great sadness, see if he appeared
strange –
in any way different. I really tried, until I could endure
it no longer. I hid behind my book
then glanced across. Colin was livelier than ever he is
in science. 'Come on Gurdie,' he said, 'let's do the biz…'
They walked to the sink, Gurdip's face a mask.
I felt ashamed to look.

At break-time we played soccer like we usually do.
Gurdip joined in; we didn't know whether he would.
Minutes later, he scored a brilliant goal.
We cheered, cheered as loudly as ever we could.
Gurdip turned, stood still, and looked at us all. He knew
why we cheered like that. He knew what we were
trying to say.
Suddenly, he sat down on the damp, muddy ground
and started to cry. He cried and cried, yet made no sound.
Someone ran to get Mr. Brown. Straightway
he knelt down by Gurdip, said nothing, but put an
arm round his shoulder.
I knew that Gurdip and all the rest of us suddenly
felt much older.
As we stood and watched, we thought about our
own moms and dads.
We were all very quiet.
Gurdip's day had made everyone a little sad.

SWIMMING LESSON

Usually, I love swimming.
But today I made the big mistake
of listening to the weather forecast.
'Minus temperatures… cold winds… freezing…'
All this was more than I could take.

'Mom,' I spoke quietly.
'Remember yesterday's pie?
Well, I don't think it agreed with me.
I was really ill during the night. Thought I might die.'
Mom gave me one of her looks.
'Mmm,' she said, 'clearly aqua–itis.
It's common on cold days like this.
Never mind. It's not exactly a crisis.
Fortunately, the treatment is really simple,
fun too – in fact, a load of laughs.
The only cure for you, my lad,
is a trip to the swimming baths.'
I turned slightly red.
Knees shook, eyes twitched, heart jerked.
I knew it wasn't worth saying any more.
My plan hadn't worked.

The journey to school was terrible.
The wind was from Russia; I'm certain.
It ignored every stitch of clothing. It felt like
I'd no coat, jacket or shirt on.
Then it started – horizontal rain:
first like pins, then daggers, then spears.
Like millions of insects it stung
hands, nose, cheeks, ears.
By the time I'd reached the classroom
I felt as though I'd been in a freezer,
left there for about a week,
then pulped through a lemon squeezer.
I felt even worse seconds later,
felt I was being choked,
when I looked round and saw how many
were standing by Sir's desk, clutching notes.

When Sir called the swimming register,
excuses came thick and fast.
Sir really enjoyed them. He read them out aloud,
entertained the whole of the class.
'The dog has chewed up her costume…'
'Last night the baby kept us all awake…'
'I put his trunks in the oven to dry
and forgot them when I cooked the steak…'
'Isn't it strange,' said Sir with a smile,
'that disasters like these occur
only when the temperature falls very low
and there's a hint of snow in the air?'

The coach to the baths seemed weird;
as echoey as the school loos.
'I could get used to this,' smiled Sir,
'just sitting here admiring the views…'
The changing room was draughtier than ever.
Hurricanes tore through every crack.
The showers were like Arctic seas.
I was wishing I'd brought my mac.
'What a small, exclusive group we are!'
the instructor said cheerfully.
'We'll get lots of work done here today,
turn you all into champions – just you see!'
My thoughts were far from championships.
I was quickly turning blue.
'Before this lesson ends,' I thought,
'I'll go down with some terrible "flu".'

When we jumped in the pool, what a shock we had!
The water seemed almost hot!
We felt like potatoes
bobbing round in a giant cooking pot.
We dived. We swam through legs and hoops –
some sunken, some floating on top.
We swam in pyjamas, pullovers, socks;
had a great time, till Sir called 'Stop!'
We couldn't believe that the time had gone.
'An excellent lesson!' Sir said.
'Well done Jason. Not only your green
badge have you won, but your blue *and* your red!'

I rushed into school with my terrific news,
but stopped dead when I heard 'Question one...'
The others were having a fractions test!
What a bonus! Good old Mom!

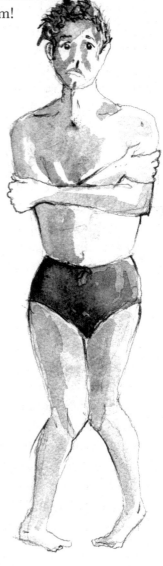

MR. CAPEWELL

I pushed at the gate, reluctant with rust.
The cratered paint was a reptile in my hand.
It was cold.
Hidden in a secret corner of the playground the sun never touched,
this gate led to a foreign land.
'Stay well away,' we were always told.
Steps, the colour of low cloud,
damp walls green with slime,
scurrying things, that brought shadows alive;

puddles, black as tar, lapped my feet,
as into dungeon, tomb, cell, mine,
or subterranean cave I dived.
Ahead of me, a tall door
blank as my breakfast mind,
pushed me backwards.
I knocked.
'Yes?' a voice called gruff and muffled.
I crept in, fearful of what I might find.
Machinery hummed. In oily shadows a figure
rocked.
Visible only by his newspaper, he sat, distant, dark,
aloof.
'Please, Mr. Capewell, could you get our ball off the
roof?'

CHRISTMAS IN YEAR SIX

It seems to me at Christmastime
the outside and inside worlds combine.
Lights, usually hanging from ceilings overhead
are seen in towns and gardens instead.
While, inside, we have branches and berries,
and words like "Noël", "Yule", and "merry"
begin to be heard once more.

Christmas in school is best of all.
The place transformed like Cinders at the ball.
It's like looking in the rear-view mirror of a car
at school, seeing familiar Christmases glimpsed from
afar,
activities remembered from years before
still happening now – though behind smaller doors.
Smartie-eyed snowmen with cotton wool snow,
wearing liquorice hats and a pasta bow,
and calendars to take home to mom.
Corridors and classrooms sparkle and gleam
with foil and tinsel. From walls stream
garlands and chains of twisted paper;
bows and flowers of cellophane and crepe or
icicles and snowflakes of enormous size –
how we hope the real thing might materialise

and turn the whole world paper-white!
In Year Six, things get more complicated:
'technological', Sir says, 'NC* related.'
Cards pop up, or turn or twist,
2D decorations hardly exist.
Mom and Dad get a Santa with sweets in his sack,
and their calendar's a snail with a shell on his back
that revolves.

We've made our party hats as well.
Mine's a Christmas cake. According to Mel,
because I've made it from polystyrene foam
it looks more like St. Paul's dome.
I said she was jealous because it was food
and that she'd eat the real dome if she could.
She agreed with me for once.
Well... it is Christmas after all.

In our class we've a frieze along the wall
of Bethlehem, complete with cattle stall
and life-size figures out of card that's been rolled
into tubes. Mel and I made a king all in gold,
with a turban of bandages and twisted tinsel.
'He needs a gift,' says Mel, 'I think I'll
use my lunch box. Mom won't mind.
At Christmas she's always especially kind.
Tomorrow I'll bring a hamper instead.'
When we'd finished, we stood back to admire our
king.
Then Mel, quietly, began to sing
"We Three Kings", when, suddenly
she stopped, turned round and grinned at me.
'Look at our classroom! she cried. 'We're in an
Eastern land, Jay,
with shepherds, crowns, angels: a land far away.

It's almost as if we're strangers here.
At any moment a genie on a carpet will appear
and whisk us back to school!'

For me, the biggest thrill of all
is performing our play in a parent-packed hall.
Back to school, when outside is the year's blackest
night,
with familiar rooms washed in unfamiliar light,
and teachers, who, everyday everyone knows
looking different – dressed in smarter clothes.
But Christmas turns to gold what once was just
metal,
changes everything and everyone into something
special.
Well, that's what I think anyway.
'Today,' Sir said, 'decorations home must go.
The forecasters have predicted snow.

We don't want angels with flakes on their wings
or frozen shepherds or soggy kings.'
So Mel took our Wise Man. I had the star,
and we packed ourselves into Mel's dad's car.
As we drove to my house through the first flakes of
snow,
we saw Jaswinder, head bent low,
a life-size sheep over his shoulder tipped,
edging carefully up the bank in case he slipped.
As we watched Jas battle against the wind
Mel and I looked at each other and simply grinned.
We didn't say anything. We didn't have to.
What the other was thinking we already knew.
Our class frieze seemed alive: here, now, today;
no longer long ago, no longer far away.

*NC= *National Curriculum*

ART APPRECIATION

One corner of our classroom we call "The Gallery."
Each week, Mr. Brown puts a picture on display
and asks us to look at it carefully and say
exactly what we think.
This week's picture frankly stinks.
It's called *Arrangement in Black and Grey*.
Why it's called this is hard to say
as it's a picture of the artist's mother
by somebody called Whistler.
We're supposed to ask each other's opinion.
I think it's the most boring picture I've ever seen.
It reminds me of something you see
on an old-fashioned TV screen.

'Great, isn't it?' Fat Mel said to me.
'I wish she was my gran.
She looks kind and you can
see she doesn't mind sitting there.
Well, neither would I. I'd be wondering where
my picture was going to go;
into what kind of gallery or show
and who was going to stare at it.
She's got dressed up specially. You can tell from her face –
and that sort of cap she's wearing – it's lace.
She made it herself years before
her eyesight deteriorated more.

She doesn't get out much now, I'm certain.
That's why she has flowers on her curtain.
They remind her of the countryside, where
she'd paddle in streams, plait daisies in her hair
or walk across fields enjoying the view
and that's why the painting's on her wall too.'

Then Barney wandered across the room.
'Can't get rid of this too soon
for me,' I said. 'Black and grey?
Give me bright colours any day!'
'But you couldn't have bright colours; they'd all be
wrong.'
Barney said. 'The old lady's seen nothing bright for
a long,
long time. Cataracts, you know Jay.
My gran's got them. She sees everything in shades
of grey.
And besides,' he added, 'the artist's right
to use dim colours, because, apart from her sight
it's been years since this lady had a really good time.
So black and grey reflect her life. I'm
sure that's what Mr. Whistler means. Don't you
agree?'

Then Mark came and stood by me.
'Rotten painting,' he said, 'really dull.
Who wants to look at a picture full
of boring colours and an old lady
who's so thin and hidden by shade, she's

hardly there at all?
I think it's a waste of space on the wall.
I'd rather have last week's Picasso.'
I gave Mark a look of pity and despair.
'I think,' I crowed, 'you're being unfair
Mark. Far from getting rid of it,
I consider it
a masterpiece.
The colours remind us of her dimming eyes.
And "boring" you say? I'm really surprised
to hear that, Mark. Can't you see
some parts tell us how things used to be?
The picture on the wall and the curtains' flowers
remind us – and her – of all the happy hours
she's spent. And the lace falling on to her shoulder
tells of how her hair was before she got older.
While the plainer parts of the painting show us how
unexciting the old lady's life is now.'

Mark looked really hard at me. 'Jay,'
he said, 'are you feeling OK?'

A VISIT TO ST. MARY'S

Mr. Brown said in school today,
'As the sun is shining and the weather seems set fair, it's
the perfect day to visit St. Mary's.
We'll walk there – it's not far to go.
Its building and grounds will show
you more about Victorians than anything I might say.'

When we reached the church Mr. Brown explained:
'We are visiting St. Mary's
looking for evidence. Care is
needed by everyone – respect too –
for a church is a holy place, you
must remember that.'

The church rose from the trees surrounding it
like a rocket amid smoke.
Windows, doorways, steps wore a cloak
of soot. The never-ending traffic grumbled past
while cheerful gargoyles cast
on us bewildered looks.
We turned the corner of the nave.
Distanced lorries scarcely whispered now,
as though invisible spirits would not allow
such ugly noise into their space.
Our excited voices too gradually died.
There was something special about this place.

'Look carefully,' Sir had said, 'at names, ages, occupations.'
Our fingers traced through lichen and moss
on weathered tombs, stones and cross.
Names we found that seemed strange to us:
'Aloysius, Septimus and Honoria,' our fingers read,
'died in infancy, twenty months, three days old…'
'Estella taken from us aged ten years. Receive into thy fold,
O Lord, and may light perpetual shine on her.'
All we could do was to stand and stare
in disbelief.

Suddenly, the ghosts we had wondered about
were no more.
No whispers of Halloween scares,
or sleepless nights and awful nightmares.
The children here were just like us: sisters, brothers.
We knew how their families felt – their fathers, mothers,
at their deaths.

The walk back to school was quiet.
As we walked through the door
we knew things were different from before.
We looked at our Victorian things on view –
the toys, the family portraits.
'Aloysius, Septimus, Honoria, is that you?'
we asked ourselves.

Odd Socks

'Jay, get a move on! You'll be late for school!'
Mom bellowed up the stairs.
I jumped out of bed, splashed water around,
dressed quickly and combed my hair.
I raced to the kitchen, trod on Ginger's tail,
grabbed some milk and a handful of flakes,
got my lunch, got my bag, said 'Cheers!' to Mom,
slammed the door, made the whole house shake.
Down the street I dashed, broke the record for the sprint
leaving Usain still on the line,
passed the shop, passed the church, passed the bus
crawling by,
reckoned I'd make school on time.

Ran up the avenue, jumping over cracks,
tried to catch sight of the big school clock,
slipped on a patch of goodness knows what.
Then I got a terrible shock.
I WAS WEARING ODD SOCKS!
I leaped up alarmed, stomach all of a churn,
and gazed down at my feet.
One was as green as the football pitch,
the other as red as raw meat.
'Oh no!' I wailed. 'Oh no! Oh no!
The whole class'll make fun of me!
Liam will laugh till he's aching and sore,
make my life a real misery.'
I undid my belt, pulled my trousers right down –
or as far as I decently could;
tried pulling the end down to my shoes,
but none of it did any good.
My trousers refused to stay in their place,
they riled up all crinkly and creased.
Every step that I took showed miles of sock –
twenty centimetres at least.
My trousers moved up and down, up and down,
couldn't stop them – try as I might:
red and green, red and green, my ankles flashed
like a set of traffic lights.
I thought I'd try different ways to walk:
knees together as though they were stuck.
But attempting to hide my red and green socks

earned me some really strange looks…
Next, like a couple of metal pipes,
I kept my legs totally straight.
Moving along like the Iron Man,
I walked nervously through the school gate.
Inside, the class was all silent and still.
Mr. Brown sat in his chair.
I knocked and anxiously entered the room –
every face a wide-eyed stare.
I mumbled a hasty apology
and sheepishly crept to my place.
Every eye in the room followed me closely,
big grins covered every face.
Mr. Brown, too, looked curious
as he peered over his specs.
'Jason, are you sure you're feeling well?'
he asked, as I stood by my desk.
'I don't think you are… Come here please.'
My heart sank right to my shoes.
I wanted to stay right where I was,
but how could I possibly refuse?
Casually, I glided out best as I could,
like a liner crossing a sea;
but sniggers and snorts I could hear all the way
as every eye in the class followed me.

'Now Jason,' Sir spoke quietly,
'do you need to go to the toilet?
Have you had an accident? You know what I mean…
Your underwear – have you soiled it?'
'No, Mr. Brown,' I said, embarrassed and red,
'it's just this bit of a pain.'
I prodded my stomach in several spots.
'I get it now and again.'
Sympathetically, Mr. Brown gave a nod.
Moving back, I saw Liam wink.
He lifted his nose, loudly sniffing the air,
expecting, I knew, a real stink…
I managed to stay at my desk all through break,
though I was dying to go to the loo.
I pressed my legs tight, thought of deserts and
things.
After all, what else could I do?

When the class came back at the end of play,
they bustled in cheerfully.
I wondered why; then it dawned on me,
the next lesson was PE.
My heart gave a thump. I came out in a sweat.
Could I get changed? No way!
I stayed in my seat, my legs out of sight,

wondering what Sir might say…
'Jason,' he said with a face of concern,
'I think I'd give PE a miss.
You're clearly unwell, everyone can see that,
and we don't want to take any risks.'
Phew! What a relief! I inwardly smiled.
When everyone's gone, perhaps
I'll be able to creep out to the loo I thought
before I suffer a collapse.

When all the class had left the room
leaving clothes strewn all over the floor,
quick as I dared, I moved from my desk
and glided towards the door.
Suddenly, I stopped dead in my tracks
and stared straight in front of me.
There lay a pair of bright red socks
belonging to Martin Cree.
I examined them. They were exactly the same as
mine!
Then to the loo I fled.
Back in class, I tore off my bright green sock
and swapped it for Martin's red.
The rest of the class returned from PE,
breathless, hot and pink.
'Feeling better Jason?' Sir asked. I replied with a
smile,
'The pain's gone altogether, I think.'

Then, 'Hey! Look at Mart's socks!' someone
shouted.
'One's red and the other's green!'
'So?' snorted Martin, 'it's the latest trend.
It's cool. Know what I mean?
All the best bands are now dressing like this.
Haven't you seen it on TV?'
Everyone gazed in admiration.
Everyone, that is, except me.
'I'm coming in odd socks tomorrow,'
Mark – and others – cried.
'What about you Jay?'
I glumly stared.
'I think I might have to,' I replied.

SNAIL DAY

Today was a really weird day in school. I mean *really* weird.
At five to nine, Sir walked in with a bucket.
'I know you're curious. You can come and look, it
contains all our lessons for today,
something we'll be exploring in every way:
brimming with ATs* – the day can't fail.
The subject of our study is…the garden snail.'

After "ughs" and "yuks" – which we felt we ought to do,
we realised that a really strange day hove in view.
One by one we went up to Mr. Brown's pail
and took, a little gingerly, our study snail.
When I got my specimen back to my chair
Mel's face was sporting a really terrible glare.
'Look at this!' she whinged, 'it's so small I think I'll

go and tell Sir. It's no bigger than a winkle.'
Seconds later she was back again.
I was about to ask how she'd got on, when
she suddenly snorted.
'Sir says he thinks I'm being sizest,
says the small snail might be the wisest.
Anyway, he says, who am I to moan about being small?
You, yourself,' says Mr. Brown, 'are not very tall.'
I don't think Mel understood Sir's recitation,
but decided to make the best of her situation.
'Never mind, little snail, you need some food,' she
said. 'I am going to call you Trudi
after a favourite aunt of mine.
She moves slowly – something wrong with her spine.
The doctors say that her diet is important:
she eats things like soya, bean curd and raw plants.
By the time you've had a few doughnuts, I'm certain,
little Trudi, you'll soon put a spurt on.'

'Trudi?' I scoffed. 'How do you know it's a girl? Her
nails are painted? Her hair's in curlers?
If you poke her does she start to wail?
Does she giggle a lot? Tell silly tales?'
'Take no notice, Trudi', said Mel. 'Uncle Jay
is just being daft – like he is every day.
But won't he feel a proper duff
when we've fed you up and you're fast and tough!'
Every lesson was entertaining.

Though things got a bit slimy, no one was complaining.
We drew our snails. Sir got rather irate
with Becky using hers as a kind of template.
'Stop that Rebecca right away,
or else I'll call the RSPCA.'
The weight of each snail was investigated,
the average speed calculated.
We worked out how long it would take our snail
to deliver letters for the Royal Mail,
to run a rounder, or a marathon.
Then we held races. Mel's lost. Mine won!

'Wait,' said Rick, 'till about twenty past three,
we'll have to eat them then – just you see…'
Mel shrieked in horror. 'Eat Trudi? No chance!'
'Why not?' asked Rick. 'They do in France.'
'Anyway,' I added, 'I thought you'd be glad
to eat yours after all the titbits it's had.'
It was true. Throughout the day Mel had
tried feeding Trudi all kinds of salad.

Now, lettuce and tomato, I could understand,
cheese and pickle I thought unwise.
But when Mel tried her jam doughnuts and cream
I could scarcely believe my eyes!
'I hope you don't think it'll eat that stuff!'
I said. 'It's a herbivore.'
'Rubbish!' snapped Mel, shoving its face into a bun,
'Can't you see she's asking for more?'
'You'll probably kill it with cholesterol,
clog up its arteries with cream.'
The snail retracted into its shell.
'Look there! See what I mean?'
'You're only jealous, 'cos you can't do the same
to yours. You don't have the resources.
Yours is a deprived child, while mine will grow
to be much bigger and better than yours is.'
'You're mad!' I laughed. 'Completely insane,
as mad as Alice's Hatter.
I bet, by tomorrow, your precious Trudi
is no bigger, better or fatter!'
'Okay!' roared Mel. 'The bet is on!
When she pops out again I'll measure her.
20p to who's right. Put your money up front.
Rick here can be the treasurer.'

So that's how the bet became to be made.
Mel spent the rest of the time crowing.
'Look at Trudi!' she'd say. 'Look at her now!
You can tell she's got bigger and is still growing!'

At half past three Mr. Brown announced
that the snails had worked hard all day.
They deserved to be taken home in comfort,
put in the garden and allowed to play.
We got yogurt pots, paper and lettuce,
and tucked our snails away carefully.
'When we get home,' Mel announced to hers,
'you'll have burgers and chips for your tea.'

Now, I'm not one of those kids to charge through the door
while the bell's still ringing, knocking stuff to the floor.
I suppose I'm not that well organised.
Well, I'm glad. I would have missed a big surprise.
I should explain that Mel lives next to the school,
which is handy for what she calls her "fuel".
Through the railings her mom pushes all kinds of things-
pizzas, crisps, sweets, doughnut rings.

I was still in the classroom packing my bag,
when in like a bull facing a waving rag
bursts Mrs. Morgan looking vexed and tense,
as though she's recovering from some dreadful experience.
'Oh, Mr. Brown,' she burbled, 'I went
to lay the table when – an accident –
I put the teapot down and didn't see
Trudi was there… I squashed her flat!'
'Good grief!' Sir exclaimed. 'Have you dialled 999?
If not, we must do so, waste no more time!'
'Hang on,' whimpered Mrs. M, 'it's a snail we're about.
There's no need to call an ambulance out.'
She went on, 'Mel's still in the shower,
but if Trudi's not there, there'll be a row. Her
temper's terrible. So help me Mr. Brown.
have you got another snail lying around?'
'Of course,' Sir said, pointing to the bucket.
Mrs. M dived in, found a snail, and took it.
I can't wait till tomorrow when I see Mel
and the story of poor squashed Trudi I tell…

I'd hardly set foot in school today,
when Mel greeted me with a grin.
'It's 20p. you owe me, Jay.
I told you I was sure to win.'
'I don't know what you mean,' I snapped.
'I've got something to tell you. The…'
'Stop making excuses and accept defeat,'
said Mel. 'Now come and measure Trudi.'

I should have told Mel about her mom,
but somehow I just couldn't do it.
'I think I know what brought on the spurt,' crowed Mel.
'It was the jam roly-poly and the suet.'

*ATs = *Attainment Targets [National Curriculum]*

MISS CARSON

Miss Carson is the oldest person I know.
She came into school today to talk to us about life
when she was a child.
She sat in front of class, by Sir's desk and smiled –
smiled all the time.
Her face was the colour of pages in old books.
Wrinkled and creased, it looked as though it had
been screwed up for ninety years.
Her hands lay in her lap and shook
gently.
Her eyes seemed wet with tears.

She told us of collecting coal in buckets off the tips
by the mine,
and about the first time she saw a banana – she
didn't know you had to peel it.
She spoke of baths in tubs, sharing water with her
sisters;
as the youngest, she was always last in line;
and about leaving food for neighbours on their front
step – no one would ever steal it.

But there's one thing I remember more than
anything about Miss Carson's story.
She lived in the house where she was born: all alone
now, no pets.
She had a cat once – Blackie – but no more. He
was killed, and she couldn't stand upsets
like that again.

I tried to think how "alone" would be.
No one to listen, no one to chat.
No one moving in the house except me – not even
my cat
Ginger.
"Alone" is something I really don't know.
Even when we're all in bed at night,
there's breathing, or snoring, or Ginger's collar
clinking as he prowls to and fro,
or Melanie, my sister, shouting out having one of
her nightmares.

When I'm old like Miss Carson and *my* hair is like
snow,
perhaps "alone" is something that I will know.
If I do, I hope that, once in a while,
like Miss Carson, I can still manage a smile.

When I came home today and listened to the usual
sounds,
for a short while I felt *glad* to have my sisters around.

BREAKFAST IN BED

A while ago, while staying at Gran's,
I thought, just for a treat,
I'd take them a cup of early morning tea.
What a surprise, I thought, that would be
for them to see me standing at their feet
with a tray.
But *I* was the one who got the surprise.
I can remember it clearly to this day...
There, on tables each side of the bed,
two tumblers stood.
In each one, like a couple of crabs swimming,
lay two sets of teeth – grinning
at me.
I stopped dead.
What had the dentures been doing through the
night?
What had they said?

'Lor! What a day! I'm ready for my soak!
That lunchtime beef was certainly no joke.
"10p. off at the market" I heard him say.
Well, if any more of it comes my way,
I'll bite his tongue till I draw
blood. He'll think twice next time if I make his mouth sore.'

'I wish Granny would pass the ice-cream by.
Every new flavour she simply has to try.
Banana Fudge Triple at temperatures polar
does nothing for my canine, incisor or molar;
and as for that popcorn she buys in a pot,
much more of that and I'll start to rot…'

'That stick of rock, I've never forgotten.
If I weren't made of plastic, I'd already be rotten:
eating the whole stick – and at his age too!
Next time it happens, I know what I'll do.
When he opens his mouth to bite off some more,
quick as a flash I'll jump out on to the floor.
Then, he'll tread on me and with a cry of dismay
he'll send me to the technician for a nice holiday.'

'Well, at least with some repose you're blessed.
Me? I hardly get any rest.
I dread Granny meeting folk at the shops.
If she does, her mouth simply never stops.
It's natter, natter, natter, natter;
it quite wears me out, this non-stop chatter.
The draught-intake is quite horrendous.
Have you got some kind of gag you could lend us?'

My gaze moved from teeth to the two shrunken
faces.
Then Gran opened her eyes.
'Who's that? Why! I do believe it's Jay!
And what have you got? A breakfast tray!
How kind of you! What a lovely surprise!'
'It's Earl Grey,' I stuttered, 'the tea you like most,
and two rounds of teeth – oops – I mean toast.'

NEXT YEAR
{LEAVING CHAPEL STREET PRIMARY}

Everybody keeps talking to me about "Next year..."
'Things', Mom says 'are bound to be strange:
different faces, buildings, routines;
but you'll soon get used to them and enjoy the change –
like stepping into trousers after wearing old jeans.'

Enjoy it? Of course I shall. Why not?
Mom's talk of trousers I don't understand,
it just adds to the confusion that's round about,
and the tales of worry, anxiety, doubt;
schemes that adults have plotted and planned.

Aunt Tracey's the worst.
'I remember when I first went to senior school
I was absolutely terrified.
The building seemed huge – like a castle or gaol.
I looked round at all the strangers – pale
as a ghost, I just sat on my bag and cried.'

When we visited the Academy, of course it seemed huge.
I felt like Jonah inside the whale.
But it's full of windows and light and space
with corridors wide enough for a six-lane race:
more a palace than a gaol.
'Remember, things will be different,' says Dad.
'The pressure put on you is certain to grow…'
Already there are targets in this and that,
not to mention English, Maths, Science SATS.
Pressure? What's different? I'd like to know!

The facilities at the Academy are fantastic.
Rooms of computers that stretch for miles,
and pitches big enough for buffalo to roam;
science labs where Frankenstein would feel at home,
and the teachers are great – everyone wearing smiles.

'You'll miss Chapel Street Primary' says Mom,
'But you'll make new friends.'
I hope my classmates are really cool.
If, like Barney they're brainy, spouting all the while
about megabytes, anthers and syntax, I'll
feel really thick – the classroom fool.
Of course, I'll miss CSP a bit:
the way you know everyone and they know you;
the teams, the concerts, the Christmas plays,
my mates of course, and all the ways
you're made to feel special – "a member of a crew".

Sometimes, you hear awful tales about secondary schools:
how you're turned upside down with your head in
the loo,
how they hide your books and cut your shoe-laces,
give you wrong directions to various places
so you end up in trouble.
But these tales aren't true.
They're only put about to make you feel scared.

I'll miss CSP more than I realise so Mom and Dad tell me.
I suppose it might be true what my parents say.
I think Mom's right to talk about jeans.
CSP is comfortable – if you know what I mean.
Maybe the Academy will feel the same one day.

I know I'm going to miss Mr. Brown:
his sense of fun and lively lessons,
his funny looks and terrible impressions,
his fancying himself as some kind of clown.
Perhaps I'm going to miss CSP lots –
even the maths tests! Who can tell?
I might, I suppose, even miss dear Mel –
her crumbs, her elbow, her splashes and blots.

Perhaps, for CSP, I might even shed a tear.
But I'll know the answer to that I suppose –
next year.

A MESSAGE FROM THE AUTHOR

These verses are born of thirty-plus years of teaching eleven year-olds.

They echo the happenings in classroom and outside school often reflecting not only the opinions of the children but also their language, similes and humour.

I am indebted to those children for making the thirty years so much fun and for teaching me such a lot.

Trevor Cattell